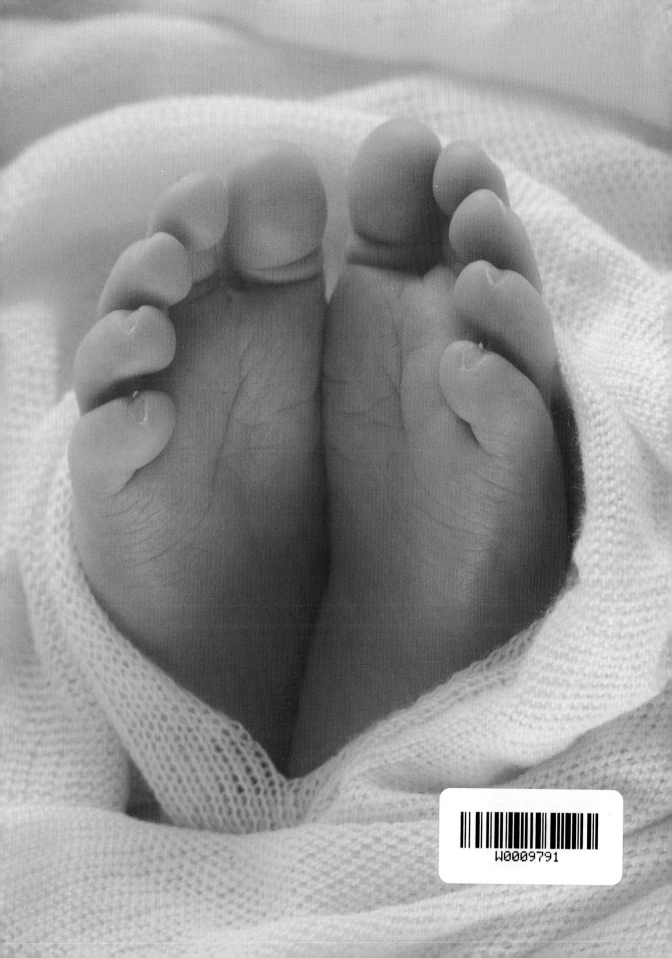

ANNE GEDDES

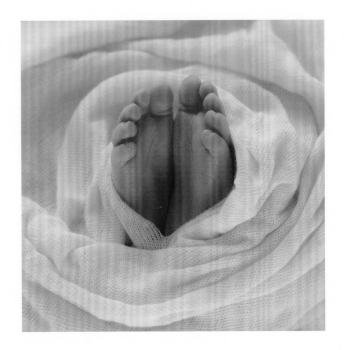

My pregnancy journal

by

_____

GEDDES GROUP HOLDINGS

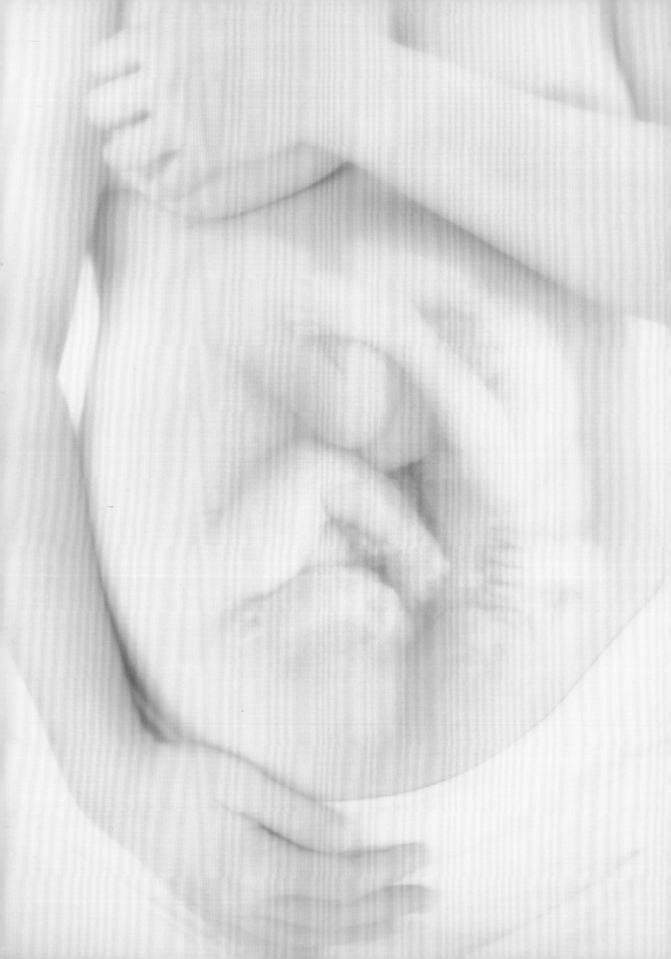

Finding out...

My story

My baby's due date

I thought I might be pregnant because

How I felt when the pregnancy was confirmed

_____

_____

_____

_____

_____

_____

Who was with me at the time

_____

_____

_____

_____

_____

_____

Children are love made visible.

American proverb

Who I shared the news with first

_____

_____

_____

_____

Their reaction, thoughts, and feelings

_____

_____

_____

_____

_____

_____

_____

_____

_____

_____

Reaction of family and friends to the news

_____

_____

_____

_____

_____

_____

People who will play an important role throughout my pregnancy

_____

_____

_____

_____

_____

_____

_____

When you were born, you cried and the world rejoiced.

Native American proverb

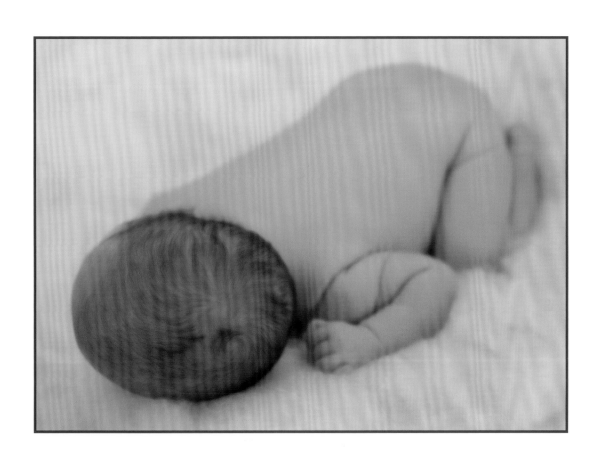

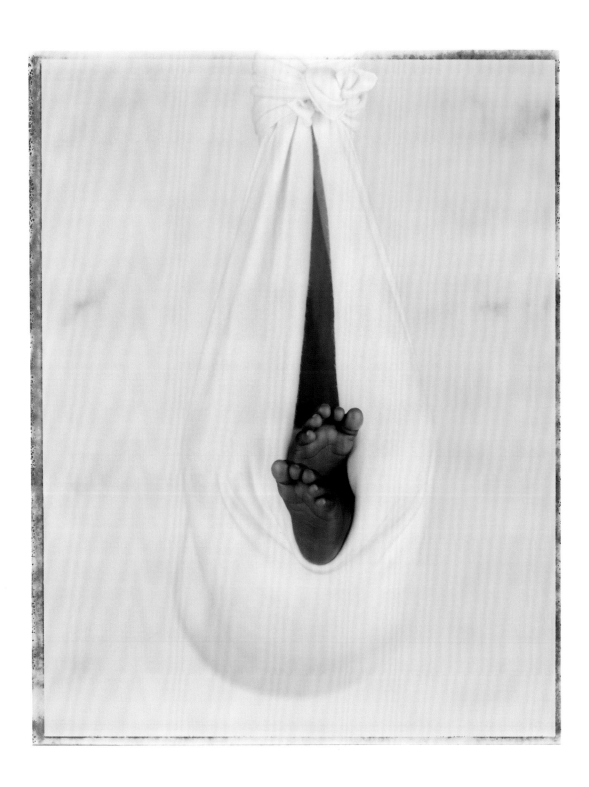

First things first

Where I would like to give birth

_____

_____

_____

_____

_____

Who I'd like to be present and why

_____

_____

_____

_____

_____

_____

_____

_____

_____

_____

_____

Mother to be

My thoughts on motherhood

_____

_____

_____

_____

_____

_____

_____

_____

My thoughts on childhood

_____

_____

_____

_____

_____

_____

_____

_____

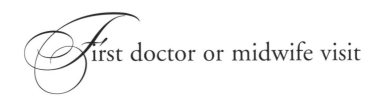

First doctor or midwife visit

Week _____

My progress _____

_____

_____

_____

_____

Baby's progress _____

_____

_____

_____

_____

Thoughts and feelings about the visit _____

_____

_____

_____

_____

_____

Mother: the most beautiful word on the lips of mankind.

Kahlil Gibran

Journey through pregnancy

weeks 1 - 12

My body

How I'm feeling about my body

_____

_____

_____

_____

_____

_____

_____

Changes I have noticed

_____

_____

_____

_____

_____

_____

_____

Cravings and aversions
_____

_____

_____

_____

_____

_____

_____

_____

Energy level
_____

_____

_____

_____

_____

_____

_____

_____

A mother's arms are made of tenderness and children sleep soundly in them.

Victor Hugo

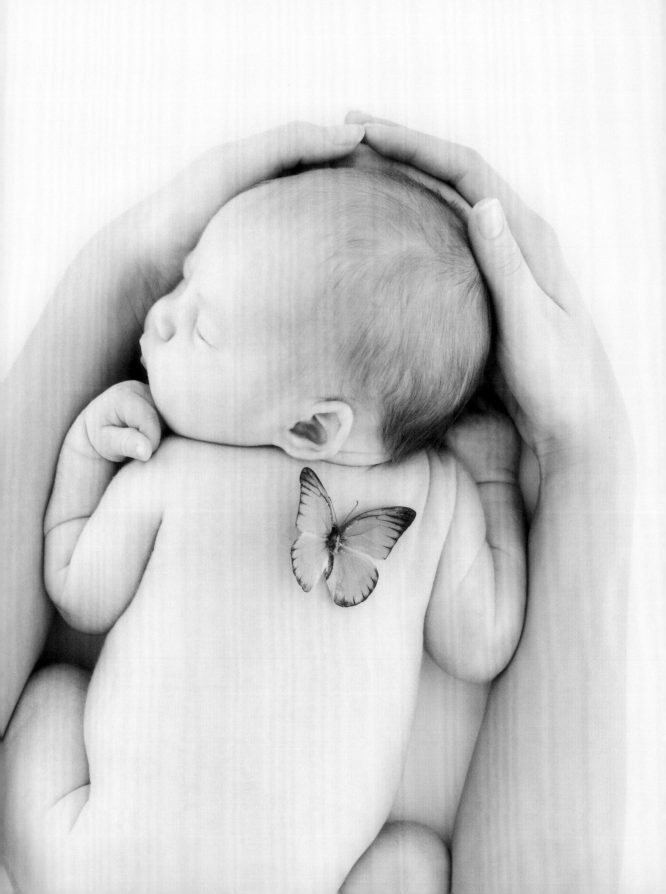

My thoughts

What I'm looking forward to

_____

_____

_____

_____

_____

_____

What I'm hesitant about

_____

_____

_____

_____

_____

_____

What makes me laugh

_____

_____

_____

_____

_____

_____

What makes me cry

_____

_____

_____

_____

_____

_____

A baby is born with a need to be loved – and never outgrows it.

Frank A. Clark

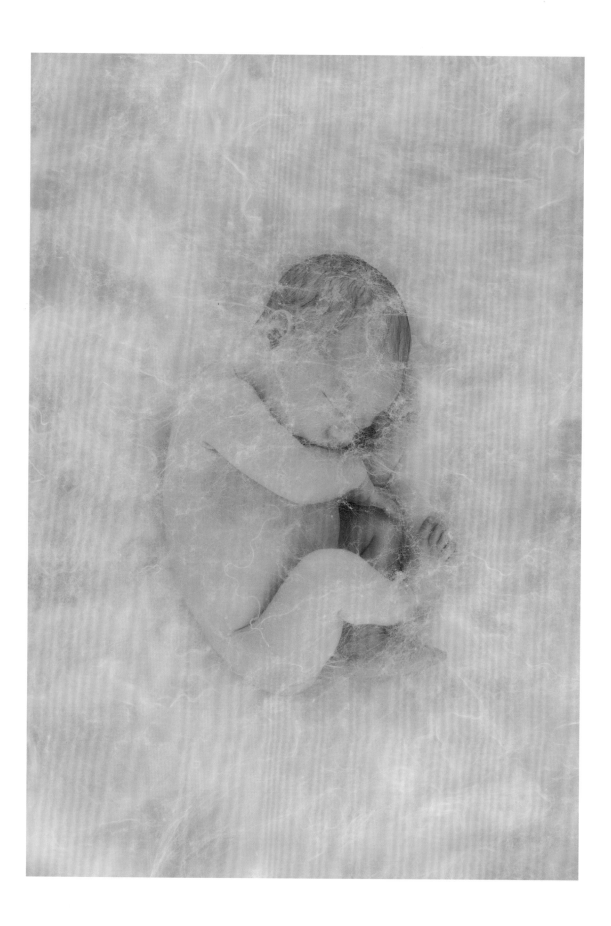

Learning

Interesting things I have learned

_____

_____

_____

_____

_____

Some good advice I received from

_____

_____

_____

_____

_____

Things to remember

_____

_____

_____

_____

_____

My disappearing waistline

weeks 13 - 24

My body

How I'm feeling about my body
_____
_____
_____
_____
_____
_____

Changes I have noticed
_____
_____
_____
_____
_____
_____

Energy level
_____
_____

What I am really enjoying about being pregnant _____

_____

_____

_____

_____

_____

But this isn't much fun _____

_____

_____

_____

_____

_____

Date _____

My weight _____   Tummy width _____

_____

It was the tiniest thing I ever decided to put my whole life into.

Terri Guillemets

27

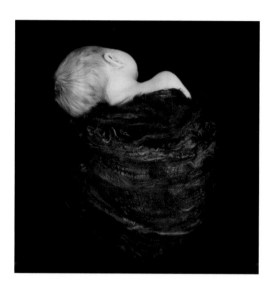
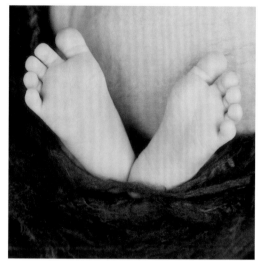
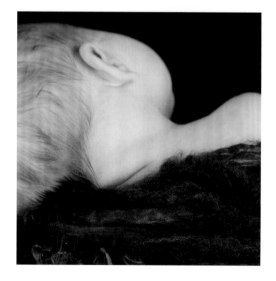
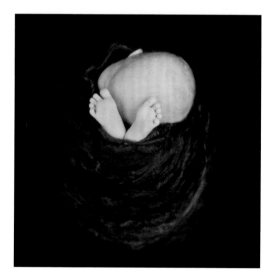

First look

Date/Week _____

Space for ultrasound

What the ultrasound shows _____

_____

_____

_____

My reaction to seeing the baby

_____

_____

_____

_____

_____

_____

_____

Reaction of others who were there

_____

_____

_____

_____

_____

_____

_____

My feelings on finding out the sex of my baby

_____

_____

_____

_____

_____

_____

_____

My feelings on having a girl

_____

_____

_____

My feelings on having a boy

_____

_____

_____

_____

Babies are such a nice way to start people.

Don Herold

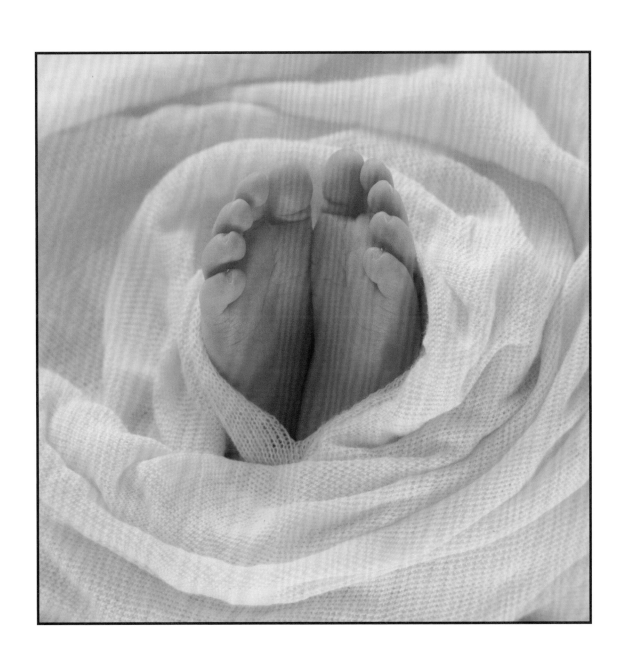

Baby's first movements

The physical feeling I had when my baby moved

_____

_____

_____

_____

_____

_____

_____

The emotional feeling I had when my baby moved

_____

_____

_____

_____

_____

_____

Doctor or Midwife visit

Week _____

My progress _____

_____

_____

_____

_____

Baby's progress _____

_____

_____

_____

_____

Thoughts and feelings about the visit _____

_____

_____

_____

Keeping up

Information I feel is important to remember

_____

_____

_____

_____

_____

_____

_____

_____

_____

_____

_____

_____

_____

_____

_____

A mother's children are portraits of herself.

Author unknown

All about me

How being pregnant is different from what I expected

_____

_____

_____

_____

_____

_____

How I am feeling about myself and being pregnant

_____

_____

_____

_____

_____

_____

Learning

I am attending childbirth classes at _____

_____

Thoughts on what I'm learning _____

_____

_____

_____

_____

_____

_____

_____

_____

_____

_____

_____

_____

_____

Information I feel is important to remember

_____

_____

_____

_____

_____

_____

_____

Friends made and their contact information

_____

_____

_____

_____

_____

_____

_____

The only thing worth stealing is a kiss from a sleeping child.

Joe Houldsworth

39

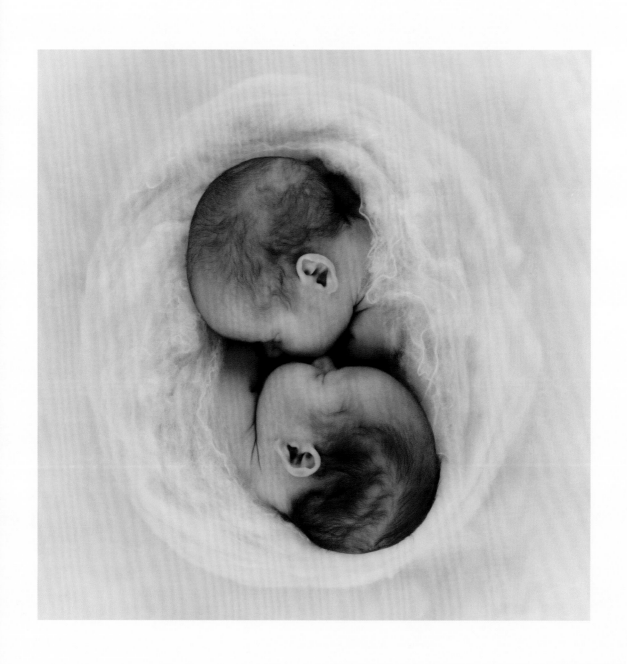

Taking care of myself

Things I'm doing now to nurture myself

_____

_____

_____

_____

_____

What I do in my time alone

_____

_____

_____

_____

Things I do to rest

_____

_____

_____

_____

What I'm reading/what I'm learning

_____

_____

_____

_____

Things I'm doing to keep myself strong and healthy

_____

_____

_____

_____

Things I'm doing to prepare my body and mind for labor and delivery

_____

_____

_____

_____

The family is one of nature's masterpieces.

George Santayana

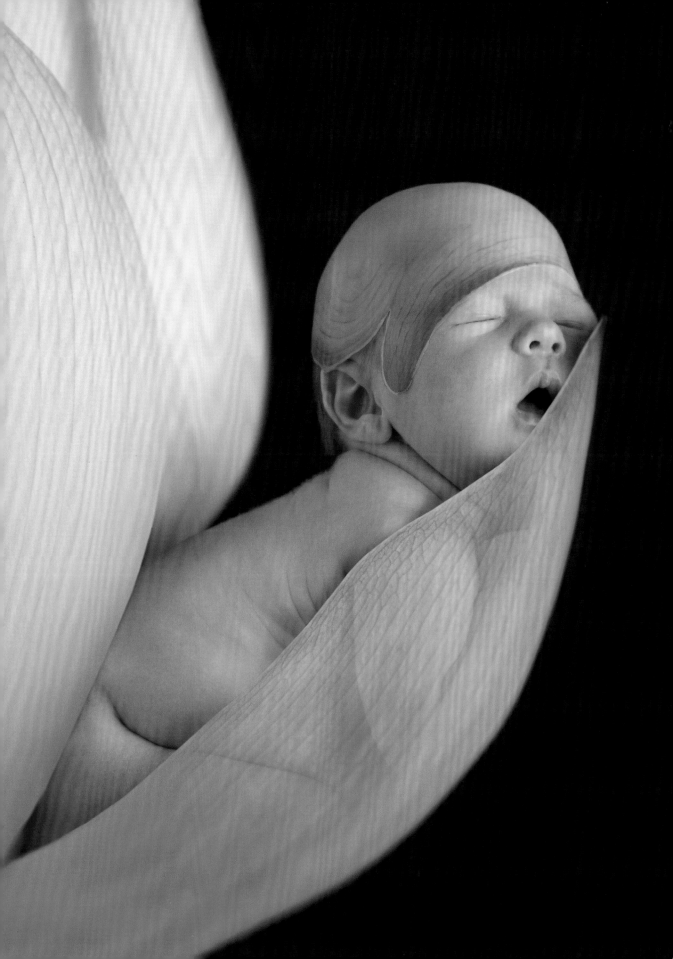

The home stretch

weeks 25 - 40

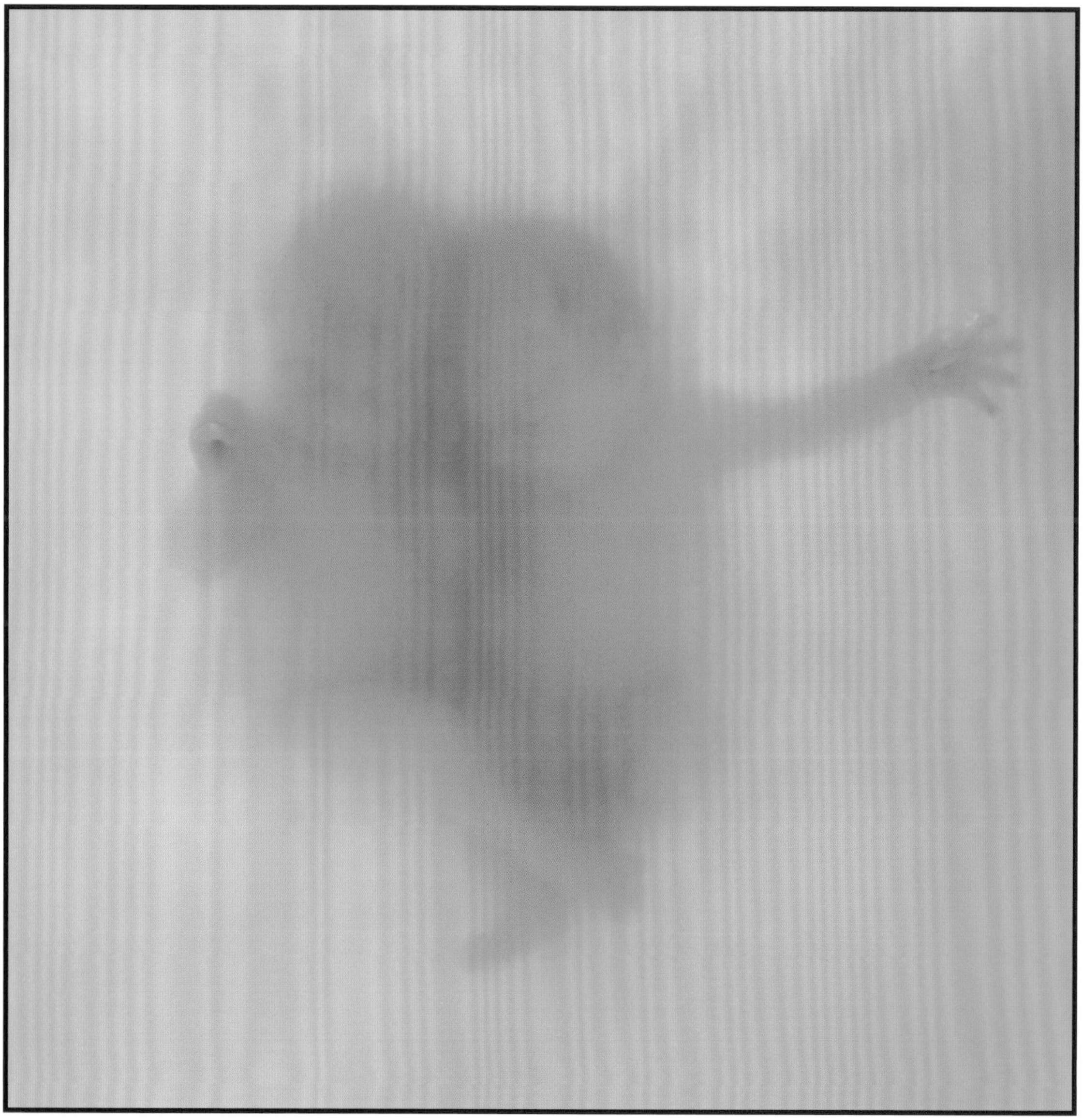

Doctor or Midwife visit

Week _____

My progress _____

_____

_____

_____

_____

_____

Baby's progress _____

_____

_____

_____

_____

Thoughts and feelings about the visit _____

_____

_____

_____

My body

How I'm feeling about my body

_____

_____

_____

_____

_____

_____

Changes I have noticed

_____

_____

_____

_____

_____

_____

Energy level

_____

_____

What I am really enjoying about being pregnant

_____

_____

_____

_____

_____

_____

_____

But this isn't much fun

_____

_____

_____

_____

_____

_____

Date

My weight   Tummy width

Babies are always more trouble than you thought – and more wonderful.

Charles Osgood

My thoughts

What I'm looking forward to

_____

_____

_____

_____

_____

_____

_____

What I'm hesitant about

_____

_____

_____

_____

_____

_____

_____

What makes me laugh

_____

_____

_____

_____

What makes me cry

_____

_____

_____

_____

Things I'm learning about myself

_____

_____

_____

_____

The soul is healed by being with children.

Fyodor Dostoevsky

Doctor or Midwife visit

Week _____

My progress _____

_____

_____

_____

_____

Baby's progress _____

_____

_____

_____

_____

Thoughts and feelings about the visit _____

_____

_____

_____

About my baby

My baby is most active
_____
_____
_____
_____
_____
_____
_____

My baby seems to respond to
_____
_____
_____
_____
_____
_____
_____

Special things I enjoy doing for my baby

_____

_____

_____

_____

_____

What I wish most for my baby

_____

_____

_____

_____

_____

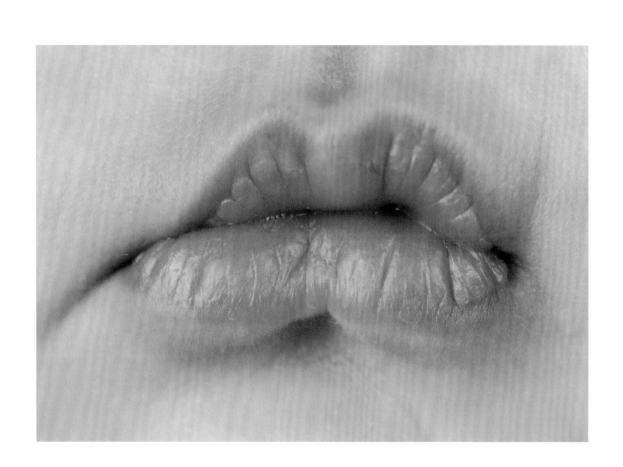

Names

Nicknames for my unborn baby
_____

_____

_____

Boy's names
_____

_____

_____

_____

_____

_____

Girl's names
_____

_____

_____

_____

_____

_____

_____

Best guesses

People's comments regarding the sex of my baby

_____

_____

_____

_____

_____

_____

_____

My own feelings about the sex of my baby

_____

_____

_____

_____

_____

_____

_____

For my baby

Special things I have for my baby
_____

_____

_____

_____

_____

_____

_____

Things I still need
_____

_____

_____

_____

_____

_____

_____

Ideas and thoughts on color/theme/feel of nursery _____

_____

_____

_____

_____

_____

_____

Gifts I have received _____

_____

_____

_____

_____

_____

_____

Little children are the most lovely flowers this side of Eden.

Rev. Dr Davies

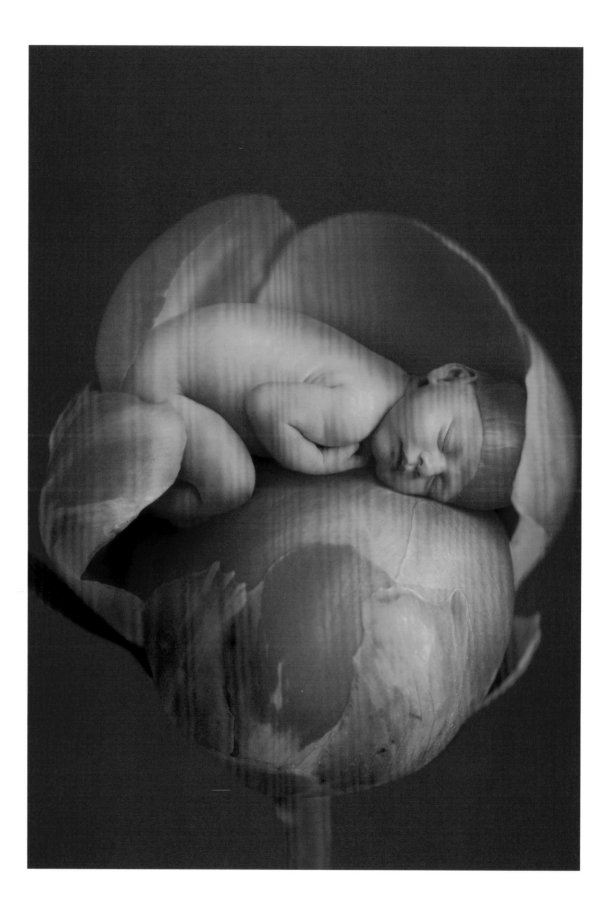

Doctor or Midwife visit

Week _____

My progress _____

_____

_____

_____

_____

Baby's progress _____

_____

_____

_____

_____

Thoughts and feelings about the visit _____

_____

_____

_____

_____

*L*ooking forward

My thoughts about giving birth

_____

_____

_____

_____

_____

_____

_____

Who I want to support me at the birth

_____

_____

_____

_____

_____

_____

_____

I am excited about
_____

_____

_____

_____

_____

I am anxious about
_____

_____

_____

_____

_____

Special things I would like to have with me at the birth
_____

_____

_____

_____

_____

Every baby needs a lap.

Henry Robin

Dreams

Date _____

Dream _____

_____

Thoughts _____

_____

_____

Date _____

Dream _____

_____

Thoughts _____

_____

_____

Date _____

Dream _____

_____

Thoughts _____

_____

_____

Doctor or *Midwife* visit

Week _____

My progress _____

_____

_____

_____

_____

Baby's progress _____

_____

_____

_____

_____

Thoughts and feelings about the visit _____

_____

_____

_____

Special note to my baby

I have been thinking about

_____

_____

_____

_____

_____

_____

I would like you to know

_____

_____

_____

_____

_____

The birth of my baby

congratulations!

My story

I knew I was in labor because _____

_____

_____

_____

_____

_____

_____

Date and time _____

Thoughts and feelings _____

_____

_____

_____

_____

_____

_____

_____

Where I was

_____

_____

_____

_____

Comments about the labor

_____

_____

_____

_____

Who was with me at the birth

_____

_____

_____

_____

_____

Love touched our hearts with tenderness anew, the day
we heard your little voice and cast our eyes on you.

Author unknown

My baby

My baby's name _____

Place of birth _____ Date and time _____

Head circumference _____ Hair color _____

Weight _____ Length _____

My first thoughts and feelings when my baby was born _____

_____

_____

_____

_____

Space for baby's first photo

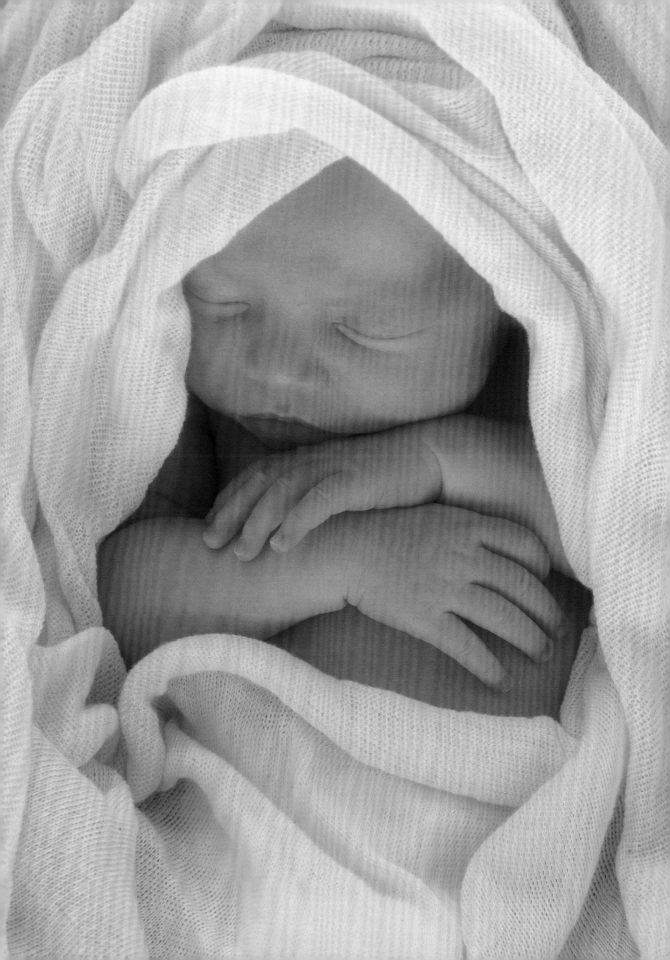

First impressions

Who cried first
_____

_____

My first words to my baby
_____

_____

_____

_____

_____

My biggest surprise about giving birth
_____

_____

_____

_____

_____

_____

_____

_____

Baby's firsts

First feeding

First bath

First diaper change

First calls to share the news

A special note to me

I feel very proud of myself because

_____

_____

_____

_____

_____

_____

_____

_____

_____

_____

_____

_____

_____

Children are likely to live up to what you believe in them.

Lady Bird Johnson

$\mathcal{J}$ust me

How my body feels since the delivery

_____

_____

_____

_____

Advice from doctor/midwife

_____

_____

_____

_____

Nursing notes

_____

_____

_____

_____

_____

_____

How it feels not to be pregnant

_____

_____

_____

_____

How it feels to be a mother

_____

_____

_____

_____

My emotions

_____

_____

_____

_____

_____

_____

Going home

Date/time _____

Baby's outfit _____

_____

How baby reacted to being home _____

_____

_____

_____

_____

My thoughts and feelings about bringing baby home _____

_____

_____

_____

_____

_____

_____

_____

_____

_____

Children are love made visible.

American proverb

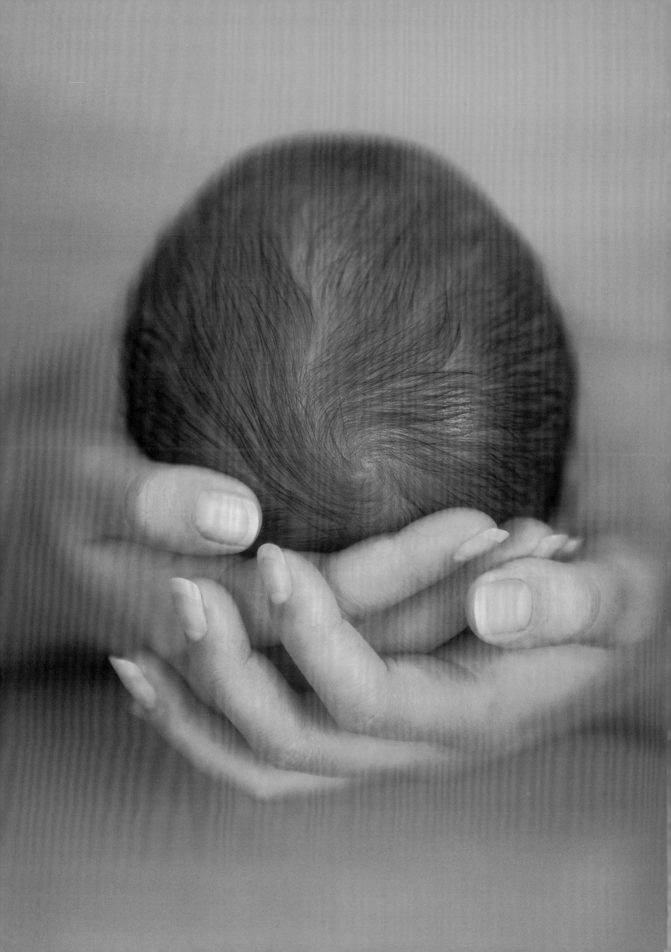

Sleeping arrangements _____

_____

_____

_____

_____

Adjusting to a new family member _____

_____

_____

_____

Memorable moments _____

_____

_____

_____

_____

_____

_____

A new baby is like the beginning of all things –
wonder, hope, a dream of possibilities.

Eda J. Leshan

Settling in

Feeding time
_____

_____

_____

Changing time
_____

_____

_____

Sleepy-time
_____

_____

_____

Baby's disposition
_____

_____

_____

Baby's visitors
_____

_____

_____

_____

_____

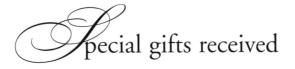

Special gifts received

In conclusion

My thoughts and feelings about finishing this book

_____

_____

_____

_____

Last words

_____

_____

_____

_____

Space for family photo

ANNE GEDDES®

www.annegeddes.com

ISBN: 978-1-921652-24-0 - Charlotte Sleeping Cover
ISBN: 978-1-921652-17-2 - Marama & Michael Cover

First published in 2008.
This edition published in 2009 by
Anne Geddes Publishing
Geddes Group Holdings Pty Ltd
Registered Office, Level 9, 225 George Street
Sydney 2000, Australia

© 2008 Anne Geddes

Designed by Kirsten Bryce
Produced by Kel Geddes
Printed in China by 1010 Printing International Limited, China